Business Success Secrets of Self-Made Millionaires

Al Rey

Smart Biz Books

DISCLAIMER

This book provides suggestions only and how the reader uses it is their choice. The authors / publishers are not liable for inappropriate use of the information by the reader.

CONTENTS

1 INTRODUCTION

This book outlines ideas, insights, and strategies that have been key to the financial success of many self-made millionaires today. These principles are all simple, effective, and relatively easy to apply. They are based on extensive research on self-made millionaires and have been proven effective time and again. Therefore, I urge you to implement them in your own life.

The advancements in science, technology, socioeconomic systems, and lifestyles have created a world where more people are achieving wealth. For example, in America, there are over five million millionaires and more than two hundred billionaires, and this number is growing by 15% to 20% each year.

Today, we have countless self-made millionaires and billionaires all over the world. This phenomenon is entirely new in human history.

The good news is that almost all of them started with either nothing or very little. Many faced financial hardship or were close to bankruptcy. Most experienced failures before finding the right opportunity for financial success. If they could do it, so can we. How? We will explore that in the following chapters.

The Law of Cause-and-Effect states that success is not accidental. Financial success comes from repeatedly doing specific things until you achieve your desired goals. The key is to ask yourself where you are headed and how you will achieve your goals while maintaining a social purpose.

Nature is inherently neutral. This means that nature, society, and the marketplace do not care about who you are, your background, or your goals. The law is simple: if you do what successful people do, you will likely get similar results. Conversely, if you do not, you will not. By accurately learning and applying the success secrets of self-made millionaires, you will achieve success, experience, results, and rewards beyond anything you have accomplished so far. You can achieve your financial dreams in a proper way.

While human nature does not fundamentally change, there are always ways to improve and develop techniques and strategies to help us overcome the significant challenge of becoming financially wealthy or a millionaire/billionaire.

For example, research suggests that in some countries, average happiness levels have not increased proportionally with growing wealth. There is no clear link between average GDP per capita and average happiness across nations. However, once a certain minimum level of income is reached, happiness tends to increase. Examples like accounting management and comparing credits and debits can significantly increase your chances of becoming a millionaire.

The key point is that you are not lesser than anyone else. You are unique, and no one can be a better version of you. There is no need for an inferiority complex. You are inherently "The Boss-Natured," capable of achieving great heights.

In fact, in-depth studies and surveys show that most self-made millionaires come from ordinary backgrounds with average education, jobs, income, and houses. However, they have learned what needs to be done repeatedly to ensure desired results. It is all about self-analysis for guaranteed outcomes.

There are 21 secrets to becoming a self-made millionaire. Each secret is crucial for achieving financial independence. Skipping any one of them could hinder your happiness and true prosperity. You can only learn these principles through repetition and consistent practice until they become second nature. You can learn and apply all these success secrets to become a self-made millionaire within your lifetime.

Now, let us embark on this journey and explore the Secrets.

2 SECRET 1: DREAM BIG DREAMS

The first secret to success is simple: Always dream big dreams. This means having boundless ambition and fostering grand dreams consistently. You should also allow yourself fantasies about the life you desire, the kind of house you envision owning, and the amount of money you would like to see in your bank account. All successful men and women began with a dream of something wonderful and grand. As the saying goes, "You have to have a dream if you want to make a dream come true."

When you start dreaming big about your success, you begin to transform your perception of yourself and your life. You take a different approach, and gradually, your life changes for the better. Dreaming big is just the beginning, but it is a fundamental secret to success.

We must also incorporate a new practice called "Thinking Back from the Future" using powerful techniques. This means adopting the powerful techniques used by influential figures who have a profound impact on your mind and behavior. Having a clear vision keeps you youthful and future-oriented, transcending the ordinary scope of life. Positive thinking, motivation, and creativity make your desires a reality.

Imagination fosters the creation of a "New Human" within you. Take the next five years to introspect and ask yourself: who are you, what are you doing, and how much are you earning? The message is clear: without ambition and imagination, nothing will materialize readily. So simply believe in yourself, you can make it.

Following this, we naturally move in the direction of our dominant dreams, images, and visions. The act of allowing yourself to dream big boosts your self-esteem and fosters greater self-like and respect. It elevates your IQ and increases your confidence level. It enhances your personal self-respect and happiness. This will make you a better person, improve your dreams, and bring them to life authentically from all perspectives.

The creativity present in big dreams is the key to achieving your goal of financial independence. The primary reason people never achieve success is because they never try. They never get started. However, when you begin to dream big about financial success, you begin to reshape your perception of yourself and life. You start doing things differently, slowly, and gradually, until the entire direction of your life changes for the better. Dreaming big dreams is the initial step towards financial success and the starting point on the journey to becoming a self-made millionaire.

Examples of Success Stories Fueled by Big Dreams

Below are examples showcasing the success stories of individuals who believed in dreaming big:

Tommy Douglas, one of the "Greatest Canadians," exemplified the power of dreaming big. He championed Medicare even when critics scoffed at his chances of success. Tommy famously said, "Dream no little dreams."

The world declared Medicare an impossibility – that Saskatchewan's budget would never be balanced, the medical establishment would fiercely oppose it, and it simply could not be done. However, Tommy persevered and achieved his goal through a dramatic team effort ignited by his courage to dream big. Fueled by this same spirit, Tommy lowered Saskatchewan's voting age to eighteen, launched a public air ambulance service, and issued a bill of rights.

This example demonstrates that when you dream big with unwavering determination, it can transform into reality.

Walt Disney harbored a grand dream of a 330-acre theme park in Anaheim, California, called Disneyland. Many considered him crazy. Even his wife was initially unconvinced about the amusement park idea. According to her, "amusement parks are so dirty," to which Walt Disney replied, "mine wouldn't be." He faced numerous rejections while seeking bank financing. He remarked that he could never convince financiers of Disneyland's feasibility because dreams offer too little security. Nevertheless, Disneyland is now a reality, and the Disney Corporation employs over 100,000 people today. This proves there is nothing wrong with dreaming big and harboring a grand vision.

Michelangelo's quote perfectly encapsulates the essence of dreaming big: "The greater danger for most of us is not that our aim is too high and we miss it, but that it is too low and we reach it."

3 SECRET 2: DEVELOP A CLEAR SENSE OF DIRECTION

Having a clear sense of direction is crucial. This means setting specific, well-defined goals in writing. Remember the saying, "You become what you think about most of the time." The two main factors that determine your life's trajectory are:

- What you think about
- How you think about it

These factors will shape your experiences based on the plans you make. In other words, successful people have clear, written goals in mind and actively work towards them. Their vision is focused on strategies for achieving these goals. They take consistent action, evaluate their progress, and focus on accomplishments instead of dwelling on worries and problems.

Successful people think about their goals constantly. As a result, they are constantly moving towards them, and in turn, their goals move closer to them. Whatever occupies your thoughts most frequently will grow and expand in your life. This is a kind of positive reinforcement. If you have a clear vision and consistently visualize your goals, you will tend to accomplish more than the average person who spends most of their time thinking and talking about worries and problems.

Acting on Your Goals

Here is a practical tip: Grab a piece of paper and start writing down your goals. The act of physically writing them down reinforces their importance. Let us say you write down 15 goals. By doing this, you will be placing yourself in the top 3% of people in your social circle. Conversely, this means 97% of people likely do not have written goals, ultimately falling behind as you act towards yours.

Prioritizing and Focusing Your Energy

Among your 15 goals, identify the one that will have the most significant positive impact on your life. Set a deadline for achieving it, create a plan, and take consistent action towards it simultaneously.

Most importantly, think deeply about that goal constantly. Talk about ways to achieve it, brainstorm different strategies to make it a reality. This exercise will act as a catalyst, sparking your creativity, increasing your energy, and propelling you towards your potential.

Example: The Power of Persistence and Positive Thinking

Consider the story of Tyler Perry, a highly successful playwright, director, producer, and actor. He has written and starred in 10 major screenplays and several movies. His work has broken box office records across America, and his plays have grossed over $100 million. Years ago, he was homeless. Today, at only 35 years old, he is a multi-millionaire.

Here is what Tyler Perry says about writing through his challenges: "I had all this negativity coming at me, and I learned that a positive word is much more powerful than a negative word always & ever."

The Science Behind Goal Setting

According to Peter Sheppard, achieving a "wide-awake" state of consciousness can be achieved through the integrated use of both left and right brain abilities. This can form the foundation for breakthroughs in personal growth and spiritual insight. These are the methods that provide you with a sense of direction – what, how, and when to do things based on your internal compass.

The practice is based on the belief that we can overcome learned limitations that restrict our actions and knowledge. We do not have to accept that we are confined by our hereditary background, childhood conditioning, or cultural influences. However, we often do not readily accept the guidance of our subconscious mind, although it has a significant impact on our thinking. There is a distinction between the conscious and subconscious mind, and both influence our thought processes.

4 SECRET 3: SEE YOURSELF AS SELF-EMPLOYED

This secret is about taking full responsibility for your actions and constantly keeping yourself engaged. It means being 100% committed and meticulous in all your endeavors. If you become unhappy with a project after starting it, it is up to you to change course and act.

Regardless of who ultimately pays you, you should always cultivate a self-employed mindset. Think of yourself as the president of your own service corporation. This perspective fosters the mentality of a responsible, self-made entrepreneur. Instead of passively waiting for things to happen, you actively make them happen. You see yourself as the captain of your own ship, in complete control of your physical health, financial well-being, career, relationships, home, car, and all aspects of your life. This is the mindset of a truly empowered individual.

In essence, self-responsible people are results-oriented. They demonstrate high levels of mental and physical initiative, making them valuable and respected assets within their organizations. They are prepared to take on positions of greater authority and responsibility in the future.

Imagine yourself as the CEO of a company for a day. You are expected to take personal responsibility for the work's outcome. Consider the changes you would immediately and progressively implement within the company. The key idea is to write down everything and make these changes step-by-step, working towards the goals outlined in a previous chapter.

Statistics Support the Self-Employed Mindset

Sources reveal that "self-employed people make up less than 20 percent of the workers in America but account for two-thirds of the millionaires."

Examples of Self-Made Success

Peter Jones: The Dragon Turned Philanthropist

Peter Jones, a prominent figure on BT (British Telecom) commercials, exemplifies the power of self-employment. He made and lost his first million in his twenties, but now ranks among Britain's 500 wealthiest individuals. Founding his first business at 17, he experienced both success and setbacks, ultimately transforming himself from a telecommunications tycoon to a renowned philanthropist. His recent success, he acknowledges, is largely attributed to "Dragons' Den," a popular television program.

President Barack Obama on Entrepreneurship

U.S. President Barack Obama recognized the importance of fostering an entrepreneurial spirit. He observed, "People have dreams, don't they? Young people have enormous vision for their futures. I think a lot of them are realizing that they won't necessarily be Robbie Williams [a pop star], but they might be brilliant businessmen and businesswomen." President Obama highlighted a key trend: "A record number, when asked what they want to be when they grow up, answer 'entrepreneur' these days. Isn't that fantastic?"

The Typical American Millionaire

Another compelling fact: a typical American millionaire is self-employed or a business owner. Among the nine million millionaires in the U.S., approximately 65% are self-employed. This group includes 4.5 million business owners and 1.5 million self-employed professionals like accountants, doctors, and lawyers.

As discussed, cultivating a self-employed mindset is essential throughout your life. Not only does it keep you actively engaged, but it also helps you develop an entrepreneurial perspective that will contribute to your overall success.

5 SECRET 4: DO WHAT YOU LOVE TO DO

This secret lies in discovering your natural talents, areas of expertise, and what you truly enjoy doing. Channel all your focus, dedication, and energy into those pursuits. Self-made millionaires have found that their strengths and abilities perfectly align with the work they do, allowing them to achieve their desired results. Many self-made millionaires often say they've "never worked a day in their life" because their passion fuels their work.

The key is to identify fields that align with your expertise, completely fascinate you, and hold your attention. Dream about a skillset or technique that naturally expresses your unique talents and abilities. This fosters a powerful flow of energy, because when you pursue what excites you, excellence naturally follows.

A self-made millionaire will relentlessly pursue what they consider their forte. They constantly strive to improve their approach to reach new heights in their chosen field. In other words, even if they won a million dollars, they would likely continue doing what they love, perhaps just in a different, better, or more advanced way. Their passion for their work is so strong that retirement would not even be a consideration.

The Importance of Passion in Work

The greatest responsibility of adult life, where you have a vast array of career and activity choices, is to identify what truly fulfills and excites you, and then actively shape your path to succeed in that field.

Examples of Passion Leading to Success

Steven Spielberg: A Lifelong Love of Film

Steven Spielberg, perhaps Hollywood's most renowned director and one of the wealthiest filmmakers globally, exemplifies the power of passion. Born in 1946, his love for film began early. Even in his pre-teens, he charged admission to show his home movies. By 12, he had completed his first production. His passion and dedication fueled his success, leading him from creating short films in his youth to becoming a Hollywood icon.

The Scrully Blotnik Study: Passion Breeds Prosperity

In 1960, psychologist Scrully Blotnik conducted a study tracking individuals pursuing wealth. He divided 1,500 participants into two groups. The larger group, with 1,245 people, prioritized getting rich first and following their passions later. The smaller group of 255 individuals believed in pursuing their passions first, trusting that financial success would follow. They embraced the "Do what you love and the money will follow" philosophy.

Twenty years later, after accounting for lost participants, the study revealed a remarkable outcome: 83 millionaires emerged from the total pool. Interestingly, only one millionaire came from the group prioritizing wealth first. The remaining 82 millionaires came from the group prioritizing their passions, trusting that financial rewards would follow.

This translates to a staggering statistic: you are 400 times more likely to become wealthy by following your passions rather than solely chasing money. The study highlights the importance of passion in driving success. When you love what you do, the dedication, creativity, and perseverance you bring to your work significantly increase your chances of achieving financial prosperity.

6 SECRET 5: COMMIT TO EXCELLENCE

Embrace Excellence and Intellectual Growth

Make an unwavering commitment to excellence and intellectual development. Resolve today to become one of the top 10% in your field. This decision can be a major turning point in your life. Relatively few people are recognized as exceptionally competent within their chosen fields. Cultivate the belief that you have the potential to be the best. Remember, everyone who excels today started somewhere. Everyone who is doing well was once a beginner.

Continuous Improvement is Key

Here is another success principle: "Your life only improves as you improve." There is no limit to how much better you can make your life by continuously learning and growing.

The Power of Excellence

Making the critical decision to pursue excellence and join the top 10% in your field is a significant turning point. It also fosters high levels of self-esteem, self-respect, intellectualism, and pride. When you are truly skilled at what you do, it instills a sense of accomplishment and boosts your confidence.

Knowing you are at the top of your game can positively impact your entire personality and your relationships with others.

Identifying Your Key Skill

The key question to consider is: "What single skill, if developed and mastered, would have the most significant positive impact on your life?"

Focus on Improvement, Not Perfection

It is unrealistic to become perfect at everything simultaneously. However, you can identify the one skill that will provide the most benefit and then dedicate yourself fully to developing it. Set this as a specific goal, write it down, establish a deadline, and create a plan to achieve it.

The commitment to excellence can significantly transform your life and propel you towards becoming a self-made millionaire over time.

Examples of Excellence

Demi Moore: Beauty and Commitment

Consider Demi Moore, selected by People magazine as one of the "50 Most Beautiful People" in the world and voted "Most Sizzling Woman" by Shape magazine readers. Despite achieving immense popularity and financial success, she continues to demonstrate a strong commitment to her acting craft, even in roles that showcase her beauty. This exemplifies dedication that transcends external validation.

The Winning Edge: Small Improvements, Big Results

Author Larry Hill introduces the concept of "The Winning Edge." This principle states that consistent, incremental improvements in your regular performance can significantly impact your results. It applies to diverse areas like horse races, golf tournaments, political elections, job promotions, and marketing. Continuously seek out opportunities to learn and refine your skills. Learn from those who excel in your field and model yourself after them. When faced with setbacks, ask yourself these two crucial questions: "What did I do well?" and "What can I do differently next time?" Learn from the successes of others and replicate their strategies. By consistently implementing these practices, you will gradually achieve similar results.

The Importance of Passion

Why is it important to do what you love? Most successful people are passionate about their work. Do you lose yourself in your work, completely absorbed in the process? Do you hold those at the top of your field in high regard? Do you find yourself naturally drawn to reading about your field and thinking about it even outside of work hours?

Do not waste your time and energy striving for excellence in something you do not enjoy. Choose a profession that fulfills you, then channel all your energy into mastering it.

Identifying Your Critical Success Factors (CSFs)

These are the essential skills and areas where you need to excel to achieve success. Typically, there are 5 to 7 key factors. Just like a chain is limited by its weakest link, your overall success can be limited by your weakest CSF.

Here is an example of Critical Success Factors (CSFs) in marketing:

- Choosing or developing products
- Crafting compelling advertising copy
- Selecting media and planning advertising campaigns
- Writing effective sales letters
- Follow-up strategies
- Business organization and general skills

- Result tracking and optimization

Failing to excel in any one of these areas can significantly impact your business.

Critical Success Factors (CSFs) in Marketing

For example, here are some Critical Success Factors (CSFs) in marketing:

Product Development and Selection: Choosing or developing products that meet customer needs and have a competitive advantage.

Compelling Advertising: Crafting advertising copy that is persuasive and effectively communicates the product's value proposition.

Strategic Media Planning: Selecting the most appropriate media channels to reach the target audience and planning effective advertising campaigns.

Sales Conversion: Writing sales letters and implementing strategies that close sales and convert leads into customers.

Effective Follow-Up: Maintaining communication with potential and existing customers to nurture leads, build relationships, and encourage repeat business.

Business Organization and Skills: Possessing strong organizational skills and a solid understanding of general business principles to manage marketing activities effectively.

Results Tracking and Optimization: Continuously tracking marketing campaign results and making data-driven decisions to optimize performance and maximize return on investment (ROI).

Failing to excel in any one of these areas can significantly impact your business's marketing success.

Seven Steps to Develop Excellence

1. **Do What You Love:** Make the conscious decision to pursue a career you enjoy. If you are not passionate about your current profession, ask yourself: "What do I truly love to do, and how can I turn it into a profitable career?" Answering these questions honestly can be one of the most important steps you take.
2. **Identify Your Critical Success Factors (CSFs):** What are the key skills that determine your level of success in your chosen field? Write them down on a piece of paper, keeping the list to a maximum of 5 to 7 factors.
3. **Assign Scores:** Rate your current skill level for each CSF on a scale of 1 to 10, with 1 being the

lowest and 10 being the highest. Be honest in your self-assessment.

4. **Choose the Weakest Link:** Identify the CSF with the lowest score. This is your area for the most significant improvement. Make a firm decision (a "quality decision") to actively improve this skill as soon as possible.

5. **Develop an Action Plan:** Set a specific goal for improving your weakest CSF, establish a deadline for achieving that goal, and create a concrete plan outlining the steps you will take to reach it.

Repeat and Refine

Once you have made significant progress on your weakest CSF, repeat steps 4 and 5 for any other CSF that scored 7 or below. This continuous process of identifying weaknesses, setting goals, and acting will help you develop well-rounded excellence in your field.

Strategic Planning Questions

Strengths Identification: Identify your strengths. What skills and abilities have you developed that you excel at? Have you specialized in a particular area, or do you need to develop additional skills to be well-rounded?

Competitive Differentiation: How do you differentiate yourself from your competitors? What do you do that sets you apart in your profession or business? This is your Unique Selling Proposition (USP). Communicate your USP clearly and effectively.

Target Audience Identification: Identify the customers, employers, or clients who would benefit most from what you do well. Once you have determined your ideal target audience, focus your efforts on attracting and serving them.

Opportunity Evaluation: Evaluate all potential opportunities and identify those with the greatest potential for success. Invest your time, energy, and resources in pursuing the most promising opportunities.

Lifelong Learning: Commit yourself to a continuous learning process. Set a goal to learn and grow consistently. This could involve reading books weekly, listening to educational audio programs, attending seminars, or taking training courses. The more you learn and develop your knowledge, the faster you will reach your goal of excellence.

7 SECRET 6: DEVELOP A POWERFUL WORK ETHIC

The Drive to Succeed

The sixth success secret is cultivating a powerful work ethic. Self-made millionaires consistently work harder and smarter than average. They build a reputation for being some of the most dedicated and sincere individuals in their fields.

The 40-Plus, Formula

The "40-Plus Formula" proposes that while 40 hours per week may ensure survival, exceeding those hours fuels success and makes dreams a reality. Working only the average of 35 hours a week will likely lead to stagnation. You will not achieve significant progress or gain the respect and financial success you desire. Every hour you invest beyond the basic 40-hour workweek is an investment in your future. The number of extra hours you dedicate to work each week can be a strong indicator of where you will be in five years. On average, self-made millionaires in America work 59 hours per week, with some exceeding 70 or 80 hours. They typically work six days a week and put in longer days, often arriving before, and leaving after standard working hours.

Focus and Efficiency

The saying "work all the time you work" emphasizes focused effort. When you are working, avoid distractions. Arrive early and immediately turn your attention to your tasks. Politely excuse yourself from social conversations or personal errands that can wait until your workday is over. Maximize your work time by staying focused and avoiding distractions. Develop a reputation for being the hardest-working and most intelligent person in your company. This dedication will attract the attention of influential individuals who can help you advance.

The Benefits of a Strong Work Ethic

A powerful work ethic goes beyond just putting in the hours. It also involves strong organizational and planning skills. Your dedication to structuring ideas logically and explaining them clearly to others builds trust in both your professional and personal relationships. You will be recognized for your capabilities and work ethic.

Examples of Dedication

Tyler Perry: Before achieving financial success and fame, Tyler Perry worked long hours in restaurants and used car lots. His dedication was such that he would sometimes sleep in his car after work.

Duncan Cameron and Simon Nixon: These entrepreneurs exemplify workaholic tendencies, often dedicating at least 16 hours a day to their dotcom business. They built a website that compares financial products, allowing customers to shop around in one place. The website generates income with every financial product sold, ultimately leading to their financial success.

Work Ethic and Self-Esteem

Judith M. Bardwick, a management consultant, observed that for workaholics, "all the eggs of self-esteem are in the basket of work." This quote highlights the potential link between self-worth and work for some individuals.

8 SECRET 7: DEDICATE YOURSELF TO LIFELONG LEARNING LIMITLESS POTENTIAL

The seventh secret to success is lifelong learning. Your potential is far greater than you might imagine. There is no problem you cannot overcome, no obstacle you cannot resolve. By applying your mind to any situation, you can achieve your goals. However, your mind needs exercise just like your body. To strengthen your mental muscles, you need to actively engage them in learning. The good news is that the more you learn, the easier it becomes to learn even more. It is like how athletic skills improve with practice. The more you devote yourself to learning, the faster you will progress and expand your knowledge base. All successful managers and leaders are lifelong learners. Make a conscious decision to become a lifelong student in your chosen field, constantly seeking new knowledge and striving to become the best.

Keys to Lifelong Learning

There are several key practices that contribute to lifelong learning:

Daily Reading: Develop a habit of reading in your field for 30 to 60 minutes each day. Reading is like exercise for your mind. An hour of daily reading translates to roughly one book per week, or 50 books per year. Over ten years of consistent reading, that is

500 books! By simply dedicating an hour each day to reading, you can become one of the most knowledgeable and highly paid individuals in your profession.

Audio Learning: Utilize audiobooks and educational programs while commuting or during any downtime you might have. The average person spends 500 to 1,000 hours per year in their car. This equates to 12 to 24 weeks, or 3 to 6 months, of working hours. Effectively, that is the equivalent of one to two full semesters at a university! Transform your car into a self-learning tool – a "university on wheels." Make it a habit to have educational audio programs playing whenever your car is running. Audio learning is often referred to as "the greatest breakthrough in education since the invention of the printing press."

Continuous Education: Take advantage of every opportunity to enroll in courses that will enhance your skills and knowledge in your field. The combination of books, audio programs, and seminars can save you hundreds of hours, thousands of dollars, and years of hard work in achieving your financial goals. Make a lifelong commitment to learning. You will be amazed at the positive impact it has on your career.

The Secret of Self-Made Millionaires

As revealed in the article "The Secret Millionaire, The Mindset Used by All Self-Made Millionaires," achieving your desired lifestyle and adopting the millionaire mindset may not be as much of a secret anymore. The popular movie "The Secret" offers insights on becoming a millionaire, living a luxurious lifestyle, and attaining your financial dreams.

Example: Phyllis Pearsall – A Lifelong Learner

Phyllis Pearsall, the eccentric British artist who single-handedly mapped London from A to Z and created a publishing phenomenon, exemplifies the power of lifelong learning. She defied the stereotype that women are incapable of reading maps, earning the (perhaps not-so-flattering) lifelong nickname "PIG." Despite a challenging childhood, she did not let that hinder her from becoming one of Britain's most fascinating entrepreneurs and self-made millionaires. Following an unhappy marriage, she needed to support herself and turned to portrait painting. It was during this time, struggling to locate her clients' homes, that her frustration with the lack of proper London maps grew. Instead of simply accepting the inconvenience, she decided to act. Remarkably, she spent a year meticulously walking and mapping all 23,000 streets of London. The success of her map led her to establish her own company, The Geographer's Trust, which continues to publish the London A-Z and maps of other major British cities.

How to Be a Millionaire in 10 Years!
The Millionaire Dream

Imagine having one million dollars saved away in a high-yield savings account in just ten years, generating enough interest to live comfortably for the rest of your life. This might seem like an impossible goal, unless you win the lottery or inherit a large sum from a distant relative. Well, it is nearly impossible, especially within such a short timeframe. However, with a little luck and a rebounding market, you might just achieve millionaire status in less than a decade.

The Numbers Game: $996 a Week

This is the approximate weekly amount you would need to invest to save one million dollars in ten years, assuming an average 12% annual return. Historically, 12% is a realistic but optimistic target.

Carving Out $996 a Week: Is It Realistic?

I admit, the heading "$996 a Week" sounds a bit daunting. We often hear about saving strategies like "making an extra $50 a month" or "cutting $20 off weekly expenses," but rarely do we hear about saving nearly $4,000 a month! If you are like me, that is a significant amount of money to set aside. So, how can the average person realistically reach this near-$1,000 weekly savings goal?

Boosting Your Savings: Multiple Income Streams
Books like "I Will Teach You to Be Rich" discuss strategies for significantly reducing expenses while increasing income. Consider creating a side hustle, a small home-based business that generates a few hundred dollars a month. Explore investment opportunities with passive income potential, such as peer-to-peer lending. You could also pursue a substantial part-time career in your off hours.

Side Hustle Income: Fueling Your Millionaire Dreams

This additional income could represent the majority of the $996 you need to reach millionaire status in ten years. Obviously, you will need to reinvest some of the profits to grow your savings, but your primary goal should be to save as much of this income as possible.

Early Mortgage Payoff: A Strategic Move

If you have a $1,000 monthly mortgage payment, paying it off early frees up that money to be directed towards your savings each month, moving you closer to your millionaire goal. Eliminating a $2,000 mortgage payment provides double the savings potential. Once your mortgage is paid off, redirect the previous

monthly payment amount towards your investments.
This single step can significantly accelerate your
wealth-building journey.

9 SECRET 8: PAY YOURSELF FIRST

The Power of Prioritizing Savings

This success secret emphasizes the importance of paying yourself first. This means prioritizing your savings and investments by consistently setting aside 10% of your income throughout your working life. Imagine receiving this 10% as an automatic addition on top of your regular paycheck, then saving it right away. For example, consistently saving $100 from each paycheck could accumulate to $1,118,000 by retirement, potentially making you a millionaire.

Building the Savings Habit

The quote, "If you cannot save money, then the foundation of greatness is not in you," highlights the importance of developing a lifelong habit of saving. It is not always easy and requires discipline, commitment, and willpower. But once saving becomes an automated habit, your financial success is more likely.

Embrace Frugality

Frugality is the practice of being prudent and avoiding waste. It is about watching every penny and making conscious spending decisions. Consider delaying non-essential purchases to allow time for reflection. This can help you avoid impulse buying.

Avoid the "Parkinson's Law" Trap

Many people retire in poverty due to frequent unnecessary purchases. They see something they like and simply buy it, falling victim to "Parkinson's Law." This law suggests that expenses tend to rise to meet your income. No matter how much you earn, you will likely spend most of it, if not a little more.

Start Small and Gradually Increase

If saving 10% of your income seems overwhelming initially, start small. Begin by saving 1% in a dedicated savings and investment account. Live comfortably on the remaining 99% of your income. As you adjust to living on less, gradually increase your savings rate to 2%, then 3%, and so on. Within a year, you could be saving 10% or even more (15% or 20%) of your income while still living comfortably. At the same time, your savings and investments will begin to grow. In a year or two, you could be in control of your finances and well on your way to becoming a self-made millionaire.

Reaching the Million-Dollar Mark by Retirement: A Case Study

Let us consider an example of how an average person, like Joe, can reach the million-dollar goal by retirement at age 67 (27 years from now). At 40 years old, Joe earns an annual gross income of $50,000. His employer offers a 401(k) plan with a matching contribution up to 5% of his salary. Joe also commits to saving an additional $4,000 a year in a Roth IRA. We have assumed a 10% annual return on his investments.

Joe's Savings Plan

Joe takes full advantage of the employer match by deferring 5% of his salary, or $2,500 each year, into his 401(k). His employer contributes an additional $2,500 each year according to the matching agreement. Assuming Joe's salary remains constant until retirement, here is a breakdown of his total contributions over the 27 years:

Account	Annual Contribution	Compounded at 10% for 27 Years
401(k)	$5,000	$605,500
Roth IRA	$4,000	$484,400

The Power of Early Starting

BUSINESS SUCCESS SECRETS OF SELF-MADE MILLIONAIRES

The table below illustrates how Joe's retirement savings would be impacted if he had started his plan at different ages. As you can see, starting to save earlier has a significant effect on the final accumulated amount:

Starting Age	Annual Investment	Annual Return	Value at Age 67
25	$9,000	10.00%	$4,838,732.00
30	$9,000	10.00%	$2,970,355.00
35	$9,000	10.00%	$1,810,239.00
40 (Joe's Scenario)	$9,000	10.00%	$1,089,900.00

45	$9,000	10.00 %	$642,624.00
50	$9,000	10.00 %	$364,902.00
55	$9,000	10.00 %	$192,458.00

The message is clear: the earlier you start saving, the greater your potential wealth accumulation thanks to the power of compound interest.

Risk and Reward: Investing for Growth When Young

When you are young, you have the advantage of time. This allows you to be a bit more aggressive with your investment selections and seek out opportunities with the potential for higher returns, like 10% or more. Forget about certificates of deposit and money-market investments – these vehicles typically will not outpace inflation. To achieve that, you will need to consider equities, or stocks.

The chart you see also demonstrates the power of compound interest, one of the most valuable tools for building significant wealth. The key is to start investing young and maintain discipline throughout your investment journey.

Madame C.J. Walker: A Case Study in Perseverance

Madame C.J. Walker's life exemplifies the value of both perseverance and saving. Born into poverty-stricken rural Louisiana, she was orphaned by the age of seven. Forced to work in the cotton fields of Delta and Vicksburg, Mississippi, to survive, she married at fourteen. After her husband's death two years later, she joined her brothers, who were established barbers. Working as a laundrywoman, she managed to save enough money to educate her daughter and even participated in activities with the National Association of Colored Women.

Through hard work, she progressed from field work to laundry services, eventually securing a kitchen cook position. Her entrepreneurial spirit, however, propelled her beyond wage-earning jobs. She leveraged her savings to launch a hair care product and manufacturing business, culminating in the construction of her own factory.

Madame C.J. Walker's story is a testament to the power of starting early. By prioritizing saving and strategically investing, even those from disadvantaged backgrounds can achieve financial success.

10 SECRET 9: BECOME AN EXPERT IN YOUR FIELD

The Rewards of Mastery

The market rewards excellence handsomely. Average performance yields average rewards, while subpar performance leads to frustration and failure. Strive to become an expert in your chosen field by diligently learning every detail and continually refining your skills.

Continuous Learning is Key

Stay Informed: Make it a habit to read industry magazines and delve into the latest books to stay abreast of current trends and knowledge.

Invest in Your Education: Attend training sessions, lectures, courses, and seminars offered by experts in your field.

Network with Top Performers: Join relevant trade or industry associations. Actively participate in meetings and connect with other high achievers in your field.

The "Law of Integrative Complexity" states that those who can effectively integrate and leverage the most information within a specific field will rise to the top. Consider salespeople, for example. The top 20% of salespeople, on average, earn 16 times more than the bottom 80%. Become a lifelong student of the sales process to excel in this field.

Building Your Own Business?

If you are starting your own business, continuously study successful business tactics and strategies. Embrace new ideas and constantly strive to improve. Set ambitious goals to become the absolute best in your industry.

Building a Complementary Team

Experts suggest that the key to a successful partnership (especially in entrepreneurial ventures) lies in having complementary skill sets. An ideal partnership often combines a strategic, introverted individual with a skilled extrovert who excels at marketing, communication, and networking. Both partners should possess exceptional skills and knowledge in their respective areas.

Example: The Allure of Online Riches

While "get rich quick" schemes may entice you, building an online business that generates millions takes time and effort. However, with dedication and the right approach, success can be achieved faster than you might imagine.

Have You Been Skeptical About Online Success Stories?

Have you heard stories about online success and thought they sounded too good to be true? Here are a few examples:

A housewife with no internet marketing experience starts making nearly $15,000 a month online within six months.

An "average" guy creates an online business selling birdcages and sells the business for $173,000 a year later.

A young father makes six figures in 12 months selling other people's products.

These stories may seem unbelievable, but they are real.

Building Your Online Success: A Streamlined Approach

I can understand your skepticism. While I achieved success myself, it took a long time. If I had known then what I know now, I could have achieved my dream life much sooner. This guide is designed to be a simplified approach to online marketing, like "Internet Marketing for Dummies!"

Here are some of the key steps covered in this guide:

Developing a Success Mindset: This is crucial for your online journey.

Finding Profitable Products: Learn how to identify winning products through reliable sources.

Attracting Customers: Discover strategies to attract potential buyers to your offerings.

Understanding Paid and Unpaid Traffic: Explore both paid and unpaid methods to drive traffic to your business.

Growth Strategies for Your Business: Learn how to implement strategies that will help your online business scale and achieve financial success.

The Importance of Details and Strategy

Each of these steps involves learning the intricacies of online business growth. By strategically implementing these steps, you have the potential to build a successful online business and generate significant profits.

11 SECRET 10: SERVE OTHERS FIRST

The Power of Service

The success you achieve in life will be directly
proportional to your commitment to serving others.
All self-made millionaires share a passion for
exceptional customer service. They prioritize their
customers' needs and constantly seek ways to improve
their offerings.

Always Ask Why

Develop a habit of asking yourself these key questions:

- What do my customers truly desire?
- What are my customers' fundamental needs?
- What constitutes value for my customers?
- How can I provide superior value to my customers
  compared to my competitors?
- What products or services are my customers
  currently purchasing from others, and what could
  I offer to incentivize them to switch to me?

Going Above and Beyond

Your success will also be significantly influenced by
what you do beyond the bare minimum. Always be on
the lookout for opportunities to exceed expectations.

Go the extra mile for your clients – remember, exceptional service does not cost extra.

Continuous Improvement: A Recipe for Success

Here is a crucial question to constantly ask yourself: "How can I enhance the value I deliver to my clients/customers today?" Continuously seek ways to add value to your services and the lives of those who depend on you. Even small improvements in customer service can significantly contribute to your financial success.

The Millionaire Mindset

Becoming a millionaire is not a "get rich quick" scheme. It requires hard work, dedication, and unwavering commitment. However, the rewards of your hard work will be substantial. Anyone can transform from ordinary to extraordinary by believing in themselves and understanding the principles that lead to success. By dedicating yourself to serving not only yourself but also others, you have the potential to join the ranks of the millionaires.

Examples of Service-Oriented Success

Arylic Singh: Sharing the Secrets of Success

"I am Arylic Singh, the sole owner of Arylic Inc. After achieving significant success, I felt compelled to share my trade secrets with all of you so that you too can achieve your dreams. Let's cultivate a spirit of helpfulness, hospitality, and knowledge sharing, just like all successful people do."

Susan Walsh: The Self-Made Entrepreneur Millionaire

Susan's Background

A lifelong entrepreneur, Susan Walsh has owned her hair salon for over twenty-seven years. For the past two decades, she is also established herself as a force to be reckoned with within the network marketing industry. Susan and her husband of 38 years, Gary, have built their dream life surrounded by their children and grandchildren.

From Workaholic to Opportunity Seeker

While Susan's story is an inspiration, her journey to success was not without challenges. Her strong work ethic, instilled in her by her father, led to a thriving hair salon that generated a six-figure income. However, Susan felt trapped. Working over 80 hours a week left her with no exit strategy and limited time with her family. She "watched them grow up through a video camera," a reality she desperately wanted to change.

The turning point came when Susan's son proudly announced his acceptance into medical school. The joy was mingled with anxiety – the additional financial burden of $5,000 a month for tuition loomed large. Suddenly open to new possibilities, Susan embraced change when presented with a network marketing opportunity through a customer interested in buying her salon for retail purposes.

"I saw a chance to sell the salon and generate more income without significantly more effort," Susan says. Intrigued, she completed the company paperwork, even if it meant driving hundreds of miles. This initial step led to an additional $5,000 per month within a short time.

Susan's Decision to Thrive

One unexpected phone call became a pivotal moment. An anonymous man inquired about Susan's experience in network marketing. Her initial response, "I'm buying wholesale and selling retail. I guess everything is going okay," belied her desire for more. The man, impressed by her work ethic and "PhD in People," offered himself as a mentor, opening doors to a world of possibilities beyond simple product sales.

"You mean I can get a percentage of what other people earn too?" Susan asked, incredulous at the concept of residual income. Recognizing her potential, the mentor offered coaching and guidance, emphasizing, "Your income growth will never exceed your personal growth."

This marked the beginning of Susan's transformation. Embracing a growth mindset, she became "hungry for knowledge." Daily self-improvement became her new mission.

The Road to Success: Challenges and Lessons Learned

Success was not immediate. Susan, like most newcomers, made mistakes and relied heavily on her mentor's guidance. Initially, she fell into common pitfalls, using a "water hose" approach, overwhelming potential recruits with product pitches. Her mentor helped her shift focus: "It's not about what you want, it's about what *they* want. People buy benefits, not products."

Susan's eagerness and willpower fueled her learning and growth. Maintaining a positive attitude and recommitting to her goals became her mantra.

Susan's Recipe for Success

Susan breaks down her business philosophy into eight key ingredients:

1. Discover the "Why"

Before someone joins your business, understand their motivations. Their "why" is the foundation for their success or failure. Are they driven by financial goals, a desire for time freedom, or something else entirely? Understanding their purpose fuels their journey.

2. Be Prepared to Hear "No"

Susan acknowledges that rejection is inevitable in network marketing. The best way to handle a "no" is to gently refocus the person on their "why." Their initial response does not define their potential.

3. Build a Personalized Business Plan

A successful business plan is customized to everyone's needs. Consider factors like available time, work ethic, commitment level, and financial investment. Ultimately, the plan should align with their "why." "Treat this like a real business, and it will reward you like one," Susan advises. "Treat it like a hobby, and it will cost you money."

4. Build Belief

Many newcomers to network marketing bring a traditional employee mindset. They expect clear instructions and immediate results. "If you help someone develop their 'three-day story' within the first

72 hours," Susan suggests, "you'll help them build belief much quicker." The "three-day story" is a concise narrative outlining their goals and the network marketing opportunity's potential to achieve them.

5. Move to Action

"Without action, there's no progress," Susan emphasizes. "No progress means no results." Inspire action by showing people how to jump-start their business.

6. Gather Testimonials

When someone joins Susan's team, she asks them to identify respected individuals in their community – "difference makers" who inspire change. These could be doctors, teachers, or other influential figures. New team members can model themselves after these respected figures.

7. Follow a Path of Exposure

Network marketing thrives on momentum. New consultants should actively participate in private businesses, chamber events, and various meetings to increase visibility. The goal is to sponsor 12 people in the first month, not the first year.

8. Embrace the System

Each new consultant should diligently follow the company's established system, a step-by-step approach to growth within the network marketing structure.

Susan's Why: A Continuously Evolving Force

Susan's "why" has grown and transformed over the years, as has her vision. "If your why isn't constantly expanding," she asserts, "how can you lead others? If your vision isn't bigger than mine, you can't lead me." Through her journey, Susan has come to realize the limitless possibilities within network marketing.

Susan's Legacy: Beyond Business

While professional success is important to Susan, her core desire is to be recognized as a loving wife and mother. Her top priority is keeping her husband happy and inspiring her children. She leads by example, fostering a supportive environment that empowers her children to make sound decisions.

Susan's ultimate legacy is to demonstrate how a businesswoman can make a positive impact on the world. She embodies kindness and the principle of paying it forward. "I want to be a pioneer in this new journey," she declares. Susan's influence has touched

lives globally, helping people embrace life and discover
their self-worth.

Building Momentum: Key to Success

Network marketing thrives on momentum. New
consultants should actively participate in private
businesses, chamber events, and various meetings to
increase visibility. The goal is to sponsor 12 people in
the first month, not the first year. By taking consistent
action and leveraging the company's system, new team
members can build momentum and achieve success.

12 SECRET 11: EMBRACE HONESTY: A FOUNDATION FOR SUCCESS

This chapter emphasizes the importance of unwavering honesty in all aspects of your life and business dealings. Developing a reputation for absolute integrity is perhaps your most asset. Always strive to be truthful in your words and actions, never compromising your ethics. Remember, your word is your bond. Success as a self-made millionaire hinge on the trust you inspire in others. People who trust you completely are more likely to:

- Collaborate with you
- Extend credit to you
- Lend you money
- Purchase your products and services, even during challenging times

Your character is the cornerstone of your life, built upon your commitment to integrity and ethical principles. Here are two key aspects of integrity:

- **Internal Integrity:** Be true to yourself in all you do. Give your best effort and remain steadfast in your values. Internal integrity translates to personal honesty and producing high-quality work.
- **External Integrity:** Be truthful and ethical in your interactions with others. Refuse to compromise your integrity for any reason.

The Power of Self-Reflection

Consider this question: "What kind of world would we live in if everyone embodied my values and behaviors?" This introspective exercise encourages you to set high standards for yourself. Ideally, you should conduct yourself as if everyone is observing your actions and potentially emulating them.

The Traits of Millionaires

Independent Thinking

Millionaires possess a unique thought process that extends beyond finances. Their thinking patterns influence their actions. Aspiring millionaires should cultivate thought processes that propel them towards their goals. Independent thinking does not imply going against the grain; it means having the courage to pursue what matters most to you. The lesson here is to forge your own path and allow your success to lead to financial rewards, not the other way around (for a deeper dive, consider reading "Getting A Millionaire's Mindset").

David Geffen: A Self-Made Success Story

David Geffen, a college dropout turned self-made millionaire with a net worth of $4.5 billion in 2009, exemplifies the power of independent thinking. This American record executive and film producer found success by founding record labels and signing iconic musicians in the 1970s and 1980s. Despite not following a conventional path, his unwavering work ethic and unwavering belief in artists' potential enabled him to amass a significant fortune.

Vision

Millionaires possess a clear, positive vision for the future. They not only dream big but also believe their dreams are attainable. Wealth seekers should set ambitious goals and embrace uncharted territory.

Bill Gates: A Visionary Leader

Bill Gates, the chairman of Microsoft (NYSE:MSFT), is a prime example of a visionary leader. This American entrepreneur, who co-founded Microsoft, played a pivotal role in bringing personal computers to the global market. Gates entered the personal computer industry in 1975 and remained steadfast in his vision. The development of Microsoft Windows in 1985 positioned him to capitalize on the surge in personal computer ownership.

Skills: Honing Your Strengths and Finding Your Passion

In his book "Think and Grow Rich" (1992), author Dennis Kimbro studied successful people to identify common traits. He discovered a focus on areas of excellence. Millionaires often partner with others to compensate for their weaker skills. If you are unsure of your strengths, ask friends and family for their insights. Utilize training and mentors to refine your existing skills. (Want advice from investment legends? Look no further!)

Billionaire investor Warren Buffett famously said, "Money is a byproduct of something I love to do very much." Enjoying your work fosters the discipline required for daily effort. People interact with money in various ways to make a living. For example, bankers often thrive on deal creation and persuading others to finalize transactions.

Finding your dream job may take time. The average millionaire does not discover it until around age 45 and typically achieves millionaire status by age 54. Kimbro's research revealed that millionaires attempt an average of 17 ventures before achieving success. So, if wealth is your goal, stop pursuing activities you dislike and focus on what ignites your passion. If you have not identified your passion yet, experiment and persevere until you find the perfect fit.

Investment: Planting Seeds for Future Growth

Millionaires demonstrate a willingness to sacrifice time and money to achieve their goals and pave a path to success. They embrace calculated risks for the opportunity of future rewards. Investment can involve acquiring securities, starting a business, or both – each path leads toward significant financial gain. The key is to start investing now.

Salesmanship: The Power of Persuasion

Millionaires excel at presenting ideas and persuading others to embrace them. Effective salespeople are undeterred by critics and negativity. In other words, they do not accept "no" for an answer. Millionaires also possess strong social skills. In fact, author T. Harv Eker, in his book "Secrets of the Millionaire Mind" (2005), analyzed data from a survey of 753 millionaires and concluded that social skills surpassed IQ in importance. Consider Donald Trump as a case study. His fame and fortune have fluctuated over the years, but his ability to sell himself – whether as a television personality or the mastermind behind a necktie brand – has consistently propelled him back into the ranks of celebrity millionaires.

13 SECRET 12: PRIORITIZATION AND FOCUSED ACTION

This chapter emphasizes the importance of prioritizing your activities and maintaining laser focus on one task at a time. This approach is a cornerstone of high productivity and performance. By effectively managing your priorities and diligently working towards your goals, you will attract the resources you need to thrive in life. This simple strategy has been the foundation for significant income, wealth accumulation, and financial independence for countless individuals and their families, including stockholders.

The key to mastering prioritization lies in your ability to identify the most critical task and dedicate your full attention to it until its completion. This represents a crucial test of your willpower, self-discipline, and character. It is not only essential but also paramount for achieving great success.

The Prioritization Formula

Here is a simple formula to guide your prioritization process:

1. **Create a Comprehensive List:** Before diving in, make a list of all your pending tasks.
2. **Prioritize Using Four Key Questions:** Assign priorities to each item on your list by considering the following questions:

- ○ **Question 1: "What Are My Highest-Value Activities?"** Identify the tasks that contribute most significantly to your work and business. What actions deliver the greatest value?

- ○ **Question 2: "Why Am I on the Payroll?"** Clearly define your core responsibilities. Focus on achieving results, not simply completing activities.

- ○ **Question 3: "What Can Only I Do That Makes a Real Difference?"** Identify tasks that are unique to your skillset and capabilities. These are tasks that will fall short of their potential if not completed by you. Conversely, your successful execution of these tasks will significantly impact your business or personal life.

- ○ **Question 4: "What Is the Most Valuable Use of My Time Right Now?"** There can only be one true answer to this question at any given moment. Your ability to identify the most valuable use of your time and immediately begin working on that task is the key to maximizing productivity and achieving financial success.

3. **Single-Minded Commitment:** Once you have identified the most important task, dedicate

yourself to completing it with unwavering focus. Persist without distractions or diversions. Push yourself to stay on task until it is 100% finished.

The Power of Consistent Prioritization

The good news is that by consistently setting goals, prioritizing effectively, and focusing on your highest-value tasks, you will cultivate a habit of high performance. This habit will eventually become second nature, propelling you towards remarkable success in life.

Example 1: Prioritization in Daily Life

"Life is a series of choices," the quote goes. "Each and every choice we make reflects our priorities." Consider the simple act of answering the phone. When the phone rings, we glance at the caller ID and decide whether to answer it ourselves or let voicemail take the call. I have encountered many people in the home-based business industry who proudly announce they do not answer their own phones. This prioritization choice, however, can have unintended consequences. Many people, in the US and elsewhere, become so engrossed in their daily routines that personal communication falls by the wayside. This can lead to missed opportunities to explore new avenues.

Example 2: The Goal-Setting Notebook Technique

This example describes a simple notebook technique purported to help you achieve millionaire status. The instructions are as follows:

1. Obtain a notebook and always carry it with you.
2. Daily, write down your ten most important goals without referencing your previous list. Repeat this process every day.

Several remarkable things are said to occur as you follow these steps. On the first day, writing your list will require thought and reflection. The second day, writing your goals without referencing the previous list will likely be a bit easier. However, the content and order of your ten goals will likely change. Some goals may appear one day and not the next, even disappearing entirely. Others may reappear at a more opportune time. With daily repetition, your goal definitions will become clearer and more concise. Eventually, you may find yourself writing down the same goals repeatedly. The order of priority may also shift as your life circumstances evolve. However, after about 30 days of consistent practice, you may start rewriting the same goals day after day.

At this point, the remarkable aspect is said to take place: your life will take off! You will feel like a passenger on a jet accelerating down the runway. Both your work and personal life will begin to improve dramatically. Your mind will be abuzz with ideas and insights. You will start attracting resources that will propel you towards your goals. Your progress will accelerate, potentially at an unsettling pace. Essentially, everything in your life will begin to transform in a positive way.

Unlocking the Power of Your Subconscious Mind: The 3P Formula

To maximize the effectiveness of this goal-setting exercise, adhere to the following "3P" formulas: Positive, Present, and Personal.

1. Positive: Your subconscious thrives on affirmative statements phrased in the present tense. Therefore, write your goals as if you have already achieved them. For example, instead of stating, "I will earn $50,000 in the next 12 months," rephrase it as, "I earn $50,000 per year." Phrases like "I will quit smoking" or "I will lose 20 lbs." should be transformed into positive statements like "I am a non-smoker" or "I weigh 150 lbs." Positive commands are essential because your subconscious mind cannot process negative commands.

2. Present: Maintain a present-tense perspective when writing your goals.

3. Personal: From this point forward, begin writing your goals in a personal manner, starting with the pronoun "I" followed by an action verb. You are the only person who can claim ownership of your goals using "I." When your subconscious receives a command that begins with "I," it is as though a production order is issued from headquarters to the factory floor, and your subconscious mind immediately goes to work to manifest that goal into reality. Therefore, begin each goal with phrases like "I earn...," "I weigh...," "I achieve...," "I win...," "I drive...," "I live in...," or "I climb..."

Supercharge Your Goals with Deadlines

To further empower your daily written goals, consider adding deadlines. For instance, rewrite "I earn an average of $5k per month" as "I earn an average of $5k per month by December 31, 2xxx." Your mind thrives on deadlines and a sense of urgency. Remember, deadlines can be adjusted as you gain new information and insights. The key takeaway is to include deadlines – they act as exclamation points, punctuating your goals with a sense of urgency and commitment.

The Power of Repetition

This exercise serves as a gauge for your true desire to achieve your goals. Often, you might write down a goal and neglect to include it again in subsequent writing sessions. This could indicate that the goal either is not a strong priority compared to others or you doubt its attainability. However, by establishing the discipline to write and rewrite your goals daily, you will gain clarity on your true desires and strengthen your belief in their achievability.

Focus on the "What," Not the "How"

When you begin writing your goals, you might not have a clear understanding of how you will achieve them. That is perfectly alright. The crucial aspect is consistent daily writing and rewriting, fueled by unwavering faith. With each repetition, you are imprinting these goals deeper into your subconscious mind.

The Subconscious Mind: Your Goal-Oriented Ally

At some point, you will start believing your goals are attainable. Once your subconscious mind accepts your goals as directives from your conscious mind, it will begin aligning your words and actions with those goals. Think of your subconscious as a powerful computer that operates 24/7, tirelessly working to bring your goals to fruition. It will start attracting people and circumstances into your life that can propel you towards your ultimate goals. Your subconscious mind is a tireless partner, working around the clock to manifest your goals into reality. Sometimes, these goals will materialize in surprising and remarkable ways.

Overcoming Doubt: Embrace the Power of Daily Goal Setting

You might encounter skepticism and doubt when writing down a new goal, questioning its achievability. The idea might reside in your conscious mind, but you have not yet developed unwavering belief and conviction in its possibility. This is a normal and natural reaction. Do not let it deter you from using this method daily.

The key to making this method work is simple: acquire a notebook and commit to writing down your 10 or so goals each day, using the positive, present, and personal tenses. That is all it takes. Within a week, month, or even a year, you will look around and witness a remarkable transformation in your life. Even if you are grasping the fundamentals of this method, dedicating just 5 minutes daily is all it takes to see results for yourself.

Boosting Effectiveness: The Power of Action Steps

Multiply the effectiveness of this method by incorporating a couple of additional techniques. First, after writing your goal in the positive, present, and personal tense, list at least 3 actions you can take immediately to achieve that goal, again using positive, present, and personal tenses.

For example, if your goal is to earn a specific amount of money, you could write: "I earn $50,000 over the next 12 months." Then, directly below, list your action steps:

1. I plan every day in advance.
2. I start immediately on my most important tasks.
3. I concentrate single-mindedly on my most important task until it is complete.

Regardless of your goals, you will be able to readily identify 3 action steps you can take right away to achieve your ultimate objectives. By writing down these action steps, you are programming them into your subconscious mind alongside your goal. At some point, you will find yourself naturally taking these steps, sometimes without even realizing it. Each step will propel you more swiftly towards your goal.

14 SECRET 13: CULTIVATE A REPUTATION FOR SPEED AND RELIABILITY

The Power of Speed and Reliability in the 21st Century

In the 21st century, "time" is a valuable currency. People today operate with a sense of urgency. Customers who were not aware of needing a product or service now crave immediate access. Patience is wearing thin across the board.

Regular customers will not hesitate to switch to a competitor who can deliver faster. Your responsibility is to cultivate a reputation for speed, a sense of urgency, prioritizing action, and swiftly capitalizing on fleeting opportunities. When a need or desire arises, move quickly. Proactively address tasks requiring attention. When a customer or supervisor assigns a task, drop everything else and complete it with such swiftness that it exceeds expectations. You have likely heard the adage, "If you want something done, give it to a busy person."

Speed Attracts Opportunities

Individuals with a reputation for swift execution tend to attract more and more opportunities to handle complex, multifaceted tasks. They are consistently presented with chances to accomplish more, faster than those who procrastinate. The ability to identify the most critical task and dedicate yourself to completing it quickly and accurately propels you to the forefront. More doors of opportunity will open for you than you can currently envision.

Example: From Dot Com to Millionaires – The Silicon Valley Phenomenon

A recent conference held in San Francisco on May 12th highlighted the professional reality that, with ever-increasing access to data and the growing demand for accurate and timely information, a focus has been placed on improving processing speeds. One approach involves developing customized data visualizations for businesses. This is a fundamental principle that can be integrated into our "Entrepreneurship Programs."

15 SECRET 14: EMBRACE THE JOURNEY: CLIMBING FROM PEAK TO PEAK

This secret emphasizes the importance of being prepared for the inevitable ups and downs of life and career. Just like a mountain climber who reaches a peak and then descends into a valley before ascending another peak, your life will follow a similar pattern. Expect a series of highs and lows – it is simply the nature of life and business. The quote "life is two steps forward and one step back" aptly captures this concept. Similarly, business life is subject to trends and cycles, much like fashion. There will be periods of growth (up waves) followed by periods of decline (down waves). These fluctuations, sometimes dramatic enough to cause industry booms or busts, are all part of the business landscape.

The ever-expanding field of Information Technology Enabled Services (ITES) has fundamentally altered many long-held beliefs and practices about how business is conducted. To navigate this evolving landscape, cultivate a long-term perspective. Develop a clear vision – a five-year plan – to guide your decisions and avoid getting swept up in the emotional rollercoaster of daily ups and downs. Remember, life moves in cycles and trends. Maintain a calm, confident, and relaxed demeanor as you navigate the fluctuations in your fortunes and opportunities. When you have well-defined goals and a daily action plan, the overall trajectory of your life will tend to be upward over time.

Example: Slumdog Millionaire: A Tale of Resilience

The critically acclaimed film "Slumdog Millionaire," based on the real-life story by Vikas Swarup and a box office hit, offers insights relevant to this concept. The movie, which garnered eight Academy Awards, depicts the harsh realities of poverty alongside the challenges faced by the wealthy (though of a different nature). Swarup introduces a diverse cast of characters grappling with various hardships, showcasing the cyclical nature of life's circumstances in India. While critics acknowledge the film's entertainment value, some find it superficial, lacking depth. Despite this criticism, Swarup's creativity is undeniable, and the movie serves as a more informative piece than a traditional novel.

16 SECRET 15: THE CORNERSTONE OF SUCCESS: SELF-DISCIPLINE

This secret emphasizes the importance of "practicing self-discipline in all things." Self-discipline is arguably the single most important quality for achieving success in life and on your path to becoming a millionaire. If you can develop the discipline to consistently do what needs to be done, regardless of your feelings, your success is practically guaranteed.

The key to becoming a millionaire lies in your ability to delay short-term emotional gratification. It is about setting a long-term financial goal of achieving significant wealth and exercising self-discipline with every expense, every single day. This discipline ensures that you only engage in activities that will ultimately lead to achieving your long-term goals.

The fundamental difference between successful people and failures boils down to habit. Successful people make a habit of doing the things that failures dislike. Interestingly, these disliked activities are often the same for both groups. However, successful people do them anyway, recognizing them as the price of admission for the success they desire. Successful people prioritize achieving the best possible results, delivered accurately and on time. Failures, on the other hand, focus on methods and techniques that provide a sense of satisfaction rather than effectiveness.

Successful people take action that directly contributes to achieving their goals. Unsuccessful people gravitate towards tension-relieving activities. Success-oriented individuals prioritize the difficult, necessary, and important tasks. Unsuccessful people prefer activities that are fun, easy, and offer immediate enjoyment or pleasure.

The good news is that every act of self-discipline reinforces subsequent acts. As you exercise self-control, your self-respect and self-esteem will naturally increase.

Life's Constant Test: Mastering Self-Discipline

Remember, life is a constant test. Every day, every hour, every minute presents an opportunity to assess your self-mastery and refine your problem-solving, decision-making, self-control, and self-discipline. The core challenge is whether you can prioritize effectively, tackle the most important tasks, and see them through to completion. The test is whether you can maintain a disciplined focus on your goals and desired outcomes, rather than dwelling on negativity or past problems. Passing this test allows you to progress to the next level. The more consistently you pass these tests, the further you will advance in life.

The article emphasizes a crucial point for aspiring high achievers: discipline is essential before transitioning from the slow lane to the fast lane.

Here is a common hurdle you will encounter: When you set your own targets and deadlines, there is no one to hold you accountable if you miss them. It is tempting to procrastinate, thinking, "I'll do it tomorrow." Here is the key: **Do everything today that you can do today!** The more you accomplish today, the more you will set yourself up for a productive tomorrow and cultivate a habit of maximizing your daily output. Conversely, if you tell yourself, you will do something tomorrow, the same excuse will likely apply the following day, leading to a cycle of laziness. While it is important to maintain a healthy work-life balance, allocating dedicated time for responsibilities, hobbies, and leisure activities, strive to maximize your productivity within those designated work periods. Discipline is paramount before entering the fast lane; otherwise, laziness can easily take hold.

What is Self-Discipline?

Self-discipline is the ability to persevere in achieving a specific goal regardless of your current environment. In a perfect world (which does not exist), everything you desire would be attained effortlessly and instantaneously. However, reality presents challenges. We live in a world where things sometimes fall short, priorities can conflict, and our energy levels may not always meet demands. This is the environment we navigate, and self-discipline equips you to overcome the setbacks it throws between you and your ultimate goals.

Building Self-Discipline: A Lifestyle, Not a Quick Fix

Developing self-discipline is undeniably an ongoing process. It is more than just a habit; it is an intrinsic quality that contributes to your overall well-being. If you cannot learn self-discipline in one area and effectively apply it to others, you might be cultivating a habit, not true self-discipline. For example, building discipline in your writing will not automatically translate to discipline in your physical fitness routine if you are a celebrity.

The key is to cultivate a specific approach that empowers you to tackle any task in any situation. Self-discipline is more akin to a lifestyle than a single, isolated activity. It is a particular personal philosophy, not just a technique you can set on autopilot and expect results.

I have personally wrestled with self-discipline for years. My inherent resistance to authority played a significant role in this. It is one of the reasons I always gravitated towards being my own boss. Furthermore, I always challenged tasks that felt imposed, making it difficult to pursue long-term goals.

However, I eventually achieved success. Running a business for ten years requires a tremendous amount of self-discipline. As you are likely aware (if you are reading this), I have also been on a raw food diet for over nine months, and as of writing this, I am on a 30-day exercise challenge. These are distinct goals – business, health, writing, and fitness – and I have made them happen.

In my experience, building self-discipline boils down to five key elements: clear goals, incentives, assessment, interference management, and opportunism. We will explore each of these one by one.

Changes made:

- Removed unnecessary phrase "after all"
- Changed "considerable" to "effectively" for better clarity
- Changed "an atomic activity" to "a single, isolated activity" for improved readability
- Changed "is more like" (repeated twice) to "It's more akin to" and "It's a particular personal philosophy" for smoother flow
- Replaced "a hell of a lot" with "a tremendous amount" for more formal tone

Clear Goals: The Roadmap to Success

Having clear goals is foundational for building self-discipline. Without a defined destination, it is impossible to accelerate your progress. Set crystal-clear goals and strive to achieve them all. One of the biggest pitfalls in maintaining self-discipline is losing sight of your objectives. You can become so engrossed in the pursuit of a goal that you forget the initial motivation behind it.

Clearly defined goals are also crucial for another reason: each goal necessitates specific actions. The actions you take to improve your health through a raw food diet will differ significantly from those required to enhance your writing skills. Self-discipline strengthens your overall strategy, but if your strategy is flawed, you will not achieve results. The lack of results can lead to discouragement and ultimately, quitting.

Incentives: Fueling Your Motivation

Building self-discipline often requires rewards to maintain motivation. While rewards are not the primary objective throughout the process, small payoffs along the way can be highly beneficial. The goal is to develop a "Swiss army knife" of self-discipline – a tool you can consistently apply in every area of your life, regardless of the specific actions or context. If rewards can accelerate the process, why not leverage them? They certainly work for me.

Most often, these rewards come in the form of simple progress assessments (we will explore assessment in more detail later). Seeing your progress and feeling good about it is a powerful motivator. When I began the raw food diet, I closely monitored my weight. Losing 7 kilograms (kg) in two months motivated me to keep going. It was like a "magical mastermind" propelling me forward. While weight loss was not the sole objective, it served as a positive reinforcement that fueled my continued efforts.

Progress Assessment: The Key to Course Correction

Self-discipline requires adjustments. Perfection is not achievable on the first try. To gauge progress and ensure you are on the right track, you need to assess your progress regularly. Consistent feedback is another fundamental element in building self-discipline. You might initially find yourself overly eager in simple situations or underperforming in challenging ones. These adjustments will gradually shape the attitude we call self-discipline.

Regardless of your specific goal, when cultivating self-discipline, do not expect immediate results. Focus on tracking your progress. Keep a record – write things on your walls, use smartphone reminders, send yourself emails – whatever method works best for you. For example, when I decided to improve my content creation speed, I also created a "blog audit WordPress plug-in" to monitor my progress.

Ignoring Distractions: Maintaining Your Focus

Even with the right goals, proper incentives, and good progress, distractions are likely to arise. I believe it is simply human nature: we tend to lose momentum just when we are gaining traction. I call these occurrences "interferences." Any time you are drawn towards something unrelated to your main goal, you are allowing an interference to disrupt your focus.

These interferences are not always negative. Fluctuating contexts can also introduce unpleasant interferences. For instance, unfinished tasks might demand your immediate attention, or a supervisor might introduce a disruptive request. Pleasant or not, you must learn to effectively ignore these interferences. Set a course for your goal and stay the course.

Opportunism: Embracing   Unexpected Advantages

Have you ever encountered unexpected luck while pursuing a goal? Perhaps unforeseen help arrived from an unlikely source, or a situational change created an unexpected advantage. These occurrences do happen. While I will not delve into the topic of attracting such serendipity, I will tell you that I am a big advocate for embracing these situations. Whenever I feel these "hidden helping hands," I reach out and take advantage of them.

Building self-discipline involves capitalizing on everything beneficial around you. If a stroke of luck appears, seize it! It will accelerate your progress. If someone offers help, accept it graciously. Do not reject it with the notion of having to do everything by yourself. Sometimes, the universe conspires in our favor, especially when we are endeavoring to implement something as challenging as self-discipline.

17 SECRET 16: UNLEASH YOUR INNER GENIUS

The good news is this: you have the potential to be a genius. You are capable of being more innovative, resourceful, and practical than you ever thought possible. Within you lies a wellspring of creative potential waiting to be tapped. It is estimated that your brain houses 100 billion cells, each intricately interconnected with up to 20,000 other cells through a complex network of neurons and dendrites. This translates to a mind-boggling number of potential combinations and permutations – far exceeding the number of molecules on our planet. This implies that your capacity to generate ideas that propel your success is virtually limitless. As a result, your potential for achievement is equally boundless.

Three key elements spark your creativity: intensely desired goals, pressing problems, and focused questions. The more you concentrate your mind on achieving your goals, tackling your toughest challenges, or seeking answers to your business and personal questions, the sharper your mind will become, and the more effectively it will serve you in the future. Think of your brain and creativity like a muscle. The more you exercise it, the stronger it becomes, with a growing capacity to handle more. By self-disciplining yourself to engage in creative thinking throughout the day, you can enhance your intelligence and even your IQ.

Remember, creativity is simply another word for "improvement." Every time you generate an idea to improve an aspect of your work, to discover newer, better, faster, cheaper, or easier ways to accomplish something, you are operating at the pinnacle of creativity.

Virgin Group: A Case Study in Creativity

I have found that the most effective way to grow any business is through creativity. The Virgin brand exemplifies this perfectly. These companies have achieved immense popularity by defying convention in some of the world's most competitive markets. In the UK, Virgin stands as one of the largest privately owned groups of companies, and their success can be attributed to their ability to rekindle excitement in somewhat dull and jaded markets. Their creative approach has garnered rave reviews for their brand and how they promote their products and services.

18 SECRET 17: SURROUND YOURSELF WITH THE RIGHT PEOPLE

The next secret emphasizes the importance of your network: "Surround yourself with the right people." Eighty-five percent of your life's success hinges on the quality of the relationships you cultivate in both your personal and professional endeavors. The more people you know, and the more people who know and hold you in high regard, the more articulate, successful, and adept at leadership you will become. Ultimately, this translates to faster progress in all aspects of your life. At every significant juncture or turning point, there will be someone who can either help you or hinder your progress.

Successful people make a lifelong habit of building and maintaining a network of high-quality relationships. This allows them to achieve far more than the average person who unwinds by watching television each night. "Everything is relationships." The challenges you face in life often stem from forming the wrong relationships with the wrong people. Conversely, virtually all your significant achievements will be accompanied by strong relationships with good people who support you, just as you support them in return. More than 90% of your success will be determined by your "reference groups" – your peers, family, and friends. In other words, your reference group is defined by the people with whom you regularly associate and identify.

You are like a highly adaptable chameleon, absorbing the attitudes, behaviors, values, and beliefs of those you spend the most time with. If you aspire to success, surround yourself with positive people. Associate with those who are optimistic, goal-oriented, and forward-moving in their lives. Concurrently, distance yourself from negative, critical, and complaining individuals. Remember the proverb: "If you want to fly with the eagles, you can't hang out with the turkeys."

Self-Made Millionaires: Masters of Networking

Self-made millionaires are lifelong networking champions. They actively participate in industry associations and attend relevant meetings. They also involve themselves in various collaborative activities. Their approach to networking is straightforward: introducing themselves to people in both business and social settings, exchanging business cards, and explaining their work.

The golden rule of networking? When you meet someone new, engage with them and learn about their business. More importantly, ask what you can do to connect them with potential clients or customers. Become a "go-giver" rather than a "go-getter." The most effective way to build relationships is to consistently seek opportunities to help others achieve their goals.

Example: The Power of Giving

Self-made millionaire T. Harv Eker offers an interesting perspective. He observes that some people in poverty believe their financial situation makes them morally superior. However, some individuals simply lack the opportunities to build wealth. If you are fortunate enough to have that ability, consider using your resources to uplift those who have not had the same advantages. In Eker's words, "Get rich and then interact and help people who do not have the opportunity you did. That makes a lot more sense to me than being broke and helping no one." Some might express concern that wealth will corrupt them. Eker argues that money simply amplifies who you already are. If you possess kindness, wealth empowers you to be even kinder. If negativity is your default, money may simply provide you with more means to be mean-spirited.

19 SECRET 18: PRIORITIZE YOUR PHYSICAL HEALTH

This secret emphasizes the importance of taking excellent care of your physical health. We are fortunate to live in an era that prioritizes physical fitness more than ever before. The goal is to reach 80, 90, or even 100 years old in excellent health, and it is achievable with determination.

Set a goal to live at least 80 years old. Then, take a critical look at your current habits. Ask yourself: will your current lifestyle enable you to reach 80 in great shape? Be honest with yourself.

There are three keys to living a long, happy, and healthy life:

The first is proper body weight management. Set a goal to control your weight and maintain a lean and fit physique throughout your life. Here is a five-word formula for weight loss and physical fitness: "Eat less and exercise more."

The second key is a proper diet. This means consuming more high-quality foods and fewer processed ones. Consider creating healthy meal plans and incorporating work-life balance programs into your routine as needed. Focus on lean protein sources, fruits, and vegetables. Minimize or eliminate sugary foods like desserts, sodas, candy, and anything else with added sugar. Explore healthy diets rich in fiber and low in cholesterol, perhaps incorporating fresh juices. Reduce your salt intake and avoid white flour products. Practice portion control and eat four or five smaller meals throughout the day instead of three large ones. Once you gain control of your eating habits, you will find it easier to manage habits in other areas of your life as well.

The Third Pillar: Exercise for Physical Fitness

The third key to a long life is regular exercise for physical fitness, aiming for 200 minutes per week, or an average of 30 minutes daily. You can achieve this by incorporating brisk walks for 30 to 60 minutes, three to five days a week. If you are serious about fitness, consider joining a gym or health club, or investing in home exercise equipment to allow for more intense or vigorous workouts.

The key to exceptional physical health and longevity lies in setting clear and specific goals for your health and fitness levels. You need to plan and then diligently follow your plan every day. This requires significant self-mastery, self-control, and self-discipline, but the rewards are extraordinary and life-changing. If your financial goal is to achieve a net worth exceeding one million dollars, your health goal should be to live as long as possible to fully enjoy a wonderful lifestyle –

the much-discussed work-life balance, a central theme of our times.

Example: The Fitness Icon Bernarr Macfadden

A Publishers Weekly article explores the life of Bernarr Macfadden, the "Muscular Millionaire," in the book titled "*Mr. America; Muscular Millionaire, Bernarr Macfadden Transformed the Nation through Sex, Salad, and the Ultimate Starvation Diet (Hardcover)*." Journalist Adams meticulously excavates the fascinating but almost unbelievable story of Bernarr Macfadden. An orphan born into extreme poverty in 1869 Missouri, Macfadden's life transformed after discovering the power of exercise. He launched a hugely successful fitness magazine called "Physical Culture," which advocated for a range of health programs that would today be categorized as alternative therapies. He is also credited with introducing the world to muscleman Charles Atlas (born Angelo Siciliano, an immigrant from Calabria, Italy).

Example: The Healthy Millionaire by Dr. Janine Bowring

A press release article dated April 19, 2009, highlights the importance of hope and faith in a prosperous and healthy future, especially in today's volatile financial market. Dr. Janine Bowring, ND, a naturopathic doctor with over 10 years of experience in detoxification of the body, mind, and spirit, offers a wealth of knowledge in her book "*The Healthy Millionaire*" on achieving a life filled with good health and abundance.

The human body accumulates external toxins and emotional burdens that can disrupt one's spirit and balance. Dr. Bowring explores how naturopathic medicine can elevate your well-being and lead to affluence through a detoxification process.

"*The Healthy Millionaire*" explains the functions of the body's major organs, guides you on refining your diet, exercising efficiently, and ridding your body of toxins and infections with the aid of naturopathic remedies and beneficial exercises.

Dr. Bowring specifically addresses:

- How to detoxify the major organs of excretion: liver, kidneys, lungs, gastrointestinal tract, and skin
- How to eliminate environmental pollutants and heavy metals from your system
- How to utilize whole foods for weight loss and longevity
- How to create wealth through the secrets of emotional and spiritual detoxification

Dr. Janine Bowring: ND, Healer, and Entrepreneur

Dr. Janine Bowring, ND, has been practicing energetic healing and naturopathic medicine since 1998, focusing on the mind-body connection and its influence on disease. She operates a medical clinic in Woodbridge, Ontario. Dr. Bowring is the formulator for Vita Tree (Trademark) Nutritionals, a whole food supplement company distributing products across Canada. Additionally, she is the founder of The Janine Bowring Foundation, a charitable organization that supports children and families in impoverished countries. Proceeds from the sale of "*The Healthy Millionaire*™" will benefit this foundation.

Dr. Bowring's "*Healthy Millionaire Secrets*" are primarily geared towards manifesting health and wealth. Leveraging her expertise as a naturopathic doctor and her role as trustee for Vita Tree Nutritionals, a whole food vitamin company, Dr. Bowring offers insights into detoxification – a practice encompassing the body, mind, and spirit – and wealth attraction.

20 SECRET 19: BE DECISIVE AND TAKE ACTION

This secret emphasizes the importance of decisiveness and action orientation. Successful people think carefully, make decisions quickly, and then act with discipline. They move swiftly, receive rapid feedback from their actions, and readily self-correct if necessary. They experiment frequently.

The other key to success is the understanding that successful people are decisive. They make quicker decisions and attempt far more than the average person. Consider the Law of Probabilities: the more approaches you try, the greater the chance of finding the one that works for you at the right time. Indecisive people, by contrast, often know what they should do or avoid, but lack the willpower or character to make firm decisions. As a result, they drift through life unfulfilled, unsuccessful, and financially dependent. They settle for far less than their potential.

When you become decisive and action-oriented, you elevate your entire life. You accomplish significantly more in a day than the average person, progressing at a much faster pace. You tap into a heightened source of energy, enthusiasm, and motivation, propelling you with joy and momentum towards your goals.

The Power of Action: Ask Yourself a Powerful Question

Here is a powerful question: "What single action, if taken immediately, would have the greatest positive impact on my results?" Whatever your answer is, do it!

Example: Millionaires in Action

Resourceful millionaires understand the importance of decisiveness and acting. How can anyone achieve wealth, freedom, or abundance if they are constantly indecisive? Millionaires do plan, analyze, and ask questions. However, once a decision is made, they act – no hesitation. They might even engage in seemingly unconventional activities, like playing the fruit machines for entertainment, viewing it as a practice run for their future endeavors.

21 SECRET 20: EMBRACE FAILURE AS A STEPPING STONE

Secret number twenty: never dwell on the possibility of failure. The fear of failure is the single greatest barrier to success in adulthood. Failure itself can make you stronger, more resourceful, and even more determined. It is the anticipation of failure, the fear that cripples your thoughts and actions, holding you back from even attempting what you need to do for significant success.

Example: The Wisdom of Thomas J. Watson Sr.

A young journalist once sought advice from Thomas J. Watson Sr., the founder of IBM, on how to achieve success faster. Watson offered these insightful words: "If you want to be successful faster, you must double your rate of failure. Success lies on the far side of failure." Embrace the journey, dare to move forward. Self-made millionaires are not gamblers, but they are willing to take calculated risks aligned with their goals to achieve greater rewards. In fact, your attitude towards risk-taking is likely the most crucial indicator of your readiness for wealth.

Whenever you face a risky situation, ask yourself this question: "What is the worst possible outcome if I proceed?" Then, follow the advice of J. Paul Getty, the self-made oil billionaire: take steps to ensure that whatever the worst outcome is, it does not happen.

The truth is, everyone experiences fear of failure, loss, poverty, and making mistakes that set them back. But self-made millionaires are those who consciously confront these fears and act anyway.

Ralph Waldo Emerson wrote, "Do the thing you fear and the death of fear is certain." When you take bold action, unseen forces will come to your aid. And each act of courage bolsters your courage and capacity for the future. Every step forward you take, even without guarantees, diminishes your fear, and strengthens your self-confidence. Eventually, you reach a point where fear no longer holds you back.

Examples of Embracing Failure

Example 1: Apollo 13: Failure Is Not an Option

Perhaps the most iconic line from the movie Apollo 13 comes from Eugene Kranz, the flight director at NASA. When everyone was on the brink of despair, fearing the loss of the spacecraft and astronauts, Kranz rallied the team with a powerful declaration: "Failure is not an option!" This unwavering focus on success, even in the face of immense challenges, exemplifies the spirit of embracing failure as a stepping stone.

Example 2: The "Millionaire Mind"

The article titled "*Millionaire Mind - Bill Bartmann - Bill Gates - Donald Trump and You* (A Big Secret of the Fact!)" explores the concept of developing a "Millionaire Mind." While various approaches exist, the article suggests that the fastest and easiest way is to directly "download" the beliefs, values, rules, attitudes, and behaviors of highly successful individuals into your subconscious mind, bypassing the resistance of your conscious mind. Once assimilated by your subconscious, you will find yourself aligning your thoughts, beliefs, and actions with those of the super-rich, ultimately leading you to take the necessary steps to achieve your financial goals. The article suggests it will feel as though you have a "magic genie" guiding you on your path to success.

Important Note: The excerpt promotes a pseudoscientific concept – subliminal messaging for wealth creation. It is important to be aware that there is no scientific evidence to support this claim.

22 SECRET 21: PERSISTENCE AND DETERMINATION: YOUR TWIN ENGINES OF SUCCESS

Secret 21 emphasizes the importance of the twin qualities of persistence and determination. Persistence, the iron will within your character, is akin to carbon in steel. Here is a crucial secret to persistence and success: program your subconscious mind for persistence well in advance of the setbacks and disappointments you will inevitably encounter on your journey to success. Resolve in advance to never give up, regardless of the circumstances. When faced with problems or difficulties, you will not have time to cultivate the necessary creativity and determination if you have not prepared for them. However, if you plan for the unavoidable ups and downs of life, you will be psychologically ready and prepared when they come. The courage to persevere in the face of adversity and disappointment is the single quality that most guarantees your success.

Your greatest personal asset will be your unwavering commitment to stay the course longer than anyone else. In fact, your dedicated effort is the true measure of your belief in yourself and your ability to succeed.

Remember, life is a continuous test of our ability to persevere. We must all pass the "persistence test." This is not a one-time exam; it is a series of pop quizzes.

You will face the persistence test whenever you encounter difficulties, disappointments, setbacks, failures, or crises in life. These challenges reveal your true character, both to yourself and to those around you.

Example: The Test of Persistence

Epictetus, the Roman philosopher, once wrote, "Circumstances do not make the man. They merely reveal him to himself." Recurring crises are inevitable in life. If you lead a busy life, you can expect to face a crisis every two or three months. Between these unavoidable crises, there will be a constant stream of problems and difficulties. The bigger your goals and the stronger your determination to become a self-made millionaire, the more problems, and crises you are likely to experience. The only thing you can control is your response to these setbacks. The good news is that every time you respond in an honest, positive, and constructive manner, you become stronger, better, and more capable of handling the next challenge that comes your way. You will become an unstoppable force, a person who never quits, no matter the problem. No matter the obstacle in your path, you will find a way to overcome it – over it, under it, around it, or through it. You will embody the relentless spirit of the Energizer Bunny from the television commercials.

Example: The Mooneys: Leaders in Overcoming Challenges

According to the resources, Matt and Ginny Mooney learned before Eliot's birth that he likely would not live long. Their story is deeply inspiring. They celebrated every single day of Eliot's life and went on to help other families with disabled children. The Mooneys are incredible leaders. They have impacted millions of people and exemplify the 7 Leadership Laws outlined in "*The Unemployed Millionaire*":

1. **The Leader Always Has a Dream Larger Than Those He or She Leads.**
2. **The Leader Always Conveys an Inspiring Vision.**
3. **The Leader Always Has a Superior (Positive) Attitude.**
4. **The Leader Sets the Bar High.**
5. **The Leader Is a Strong Decision Maker.**
6. **The Leader Has the Highest Levels of Character and Integrity.**
7. **The Leader Always Exhibits Persistence and Determination.**

This emphasizes that we all need to be leaders, not just throne rulers, to manage the millions that may come our way.

The Predictability of Success: The Most Important Message

Here is the most important message of this entire program: "Success is Predictable." Success is not a matter of luck, coincidence, or being in the right place at the right time. Success is as predictable as the sun rising in the east and setting in the west. By diligently applying the principles you have just learned, you will move to the forefront of life. You will possess an incredible advantage over those who are unaware of or do not practice these protocols and strategies. If you consistently and persistently replicate the actions of successful people, there is nothing that can stop you from achieving great success yourself.

You Are the Architect of Your Destiny

You are the architect of your own kingdom and the place of honor you occupy within it. You are the master of your own fate; that is the truth. There are no limitations on your achievements except those you impose through your thinking. You are just as good as anyone you will ever meet. You are an outstanding human being with talents and abilities far greater than anything you have ever realized or used up to now.

References

- **Dream Big and Win with Millionaire Stealth Secrets - Financial Planning** (Source: Electronic) Retrieved May 8, 2010, from A Better Family Business: http://www.abetterfamilybusiness.com

- Hang, R. (2010, January 4). Review of Secrets of Self-Made Millionaire Book by Adam Khoo. Retrieved May 8, 2010, from [invalid URL removed]

- Quote By Eleanor Roosevelt: "Friendship with oneself is all important, because without it one cannot be friends with anyone else in the world."

- "Parkinson's Law." This law states that "expenses rise to meet income. No matter how much you earn, you spend that much and a little bit more besides."

- Jacques Springer, Digratilife.com, on Personal Finance Insights from Silicon Valley on How to Be a Millionaire. Retrieved from http://www.thedigeratilife.com/how-to-be-a-millionaire

- Christian, M. (2008). "Becoming Tyler: Bill collector turned billion-dollar media mogul was molded from pain, promise and persistence." (Source not specified)

- Khoo, A. (2004). Master Your Mind, Design Your Destiny. (Source not specified)

- Moore, B. Who Wants to Be a Millionaire (Source not specified)
- Foster, W. (Source not specified). The Money Maker, Make Money Fast, Get Rich Millionaire.
- Dr. Janine Bowring, The Healthy Millionaire

www.ingramcontent.com/pod-product-compliance
Lightning Source LLC
Chambersburg PA
CBHW071228170526
45165CB00003B/1030